Alfred's **INSTRUMENTAL PLAY-ALONG**

The *Selections from* WIZARD of OZ

70th Anniversary Edition Instrumental Solos

Lyrics by E.Y. Harburg   Music by Harold Arlen

Many thanks to Marilee Bradford, Laura Lynn Broadhurst, Ned Comstock, John Fricke, and David Maxine.

Arranged by Bill Galliford, Ethan Neuburg and Tod Edmondson

Cover and page 1 photo courtesy of MGM/Photofest.
Digital photo restoration for John Fricke by Jonathan Shirshekan.

© 2009 Alfred Music Publishing Co., Inc.
All Rights Reserved. Printed in USA.

ISBN-10: 0-7390-6424-X
ISBN-13: 978-0-7390-6424-5

Contents

The Wizard of Oz: A Whiz of a Score

When M-G-M decided to produce a film musical version of L. Frank Baum's 1900 children's book *The Wonderful Wizard of Oz,* the studio's intention was for the film to have cross-generational appeal, appropriate for adults as well as children. M-G-M intended to present Baum's classic fantasy with a Broadway sensibility, utilizing the best performers of the theater and film worlds. The movie's budget was set at 1.7 million dollars, but by the time it was completed, the total had risen to 2.7 million, 65% over budget. When it was released in August 1939, it met with virtually universal acclaim, but didn't go into the black until its theatrical reissue in 1949. *Oz* didn't start reaping substantial profits until 1956, when it was first broadcast on television. Subsequent annual presentations on television, which began in 1959, helped secure the film's status as one of the best-loved motion pictures of all time.

Today, *The Wizard of Oz,* with its enchanting story and memorable songs, has become a cherished tradition in millions of households. The film's groundbreaking musical score includes a number of unforgettable classics, and is considered one of the masterpieces in film music history. Towering among the songs is "Over the Rainbow," which was named Song of the Century on a list compiled by both the Recording Industry Association of America (RIAA) and the National Endowment for the Arts in 2001. Three years later, it was selected as the number one movie song of all time for the American Film Institute's "100 Years… 100 Songs" chart. (Another song from the film: "Ding-Dong! The Witch Is Dead," came in at number 82.) The songs and the background music were primarily the work of three remarkable men: lyricist E. Y. "Yip" Harburg, composer Harold Arlen, and musical director Herbert Stothart. Together, they fashioned the memorable songs and musical themes that have remained in our collective consciousness for 70 years.

Yip Harburg

Born as Irwin Hochberg in New York's lower East Side, Edgar Yipsel Harburg (1896–1981) grew up in poverty. Along with his parents, he worked in a ladies' garment sweatshop, in addition to doing other odd jobs in the neighborhood. As a youth, Harburg fell in love with the Yiddish theater (his nickname, "Yip," was short for "Yipsl," a Yiddish term for a squirrel), and he often went to shows to laugh at the uproarious comedies and cry at the devastating tragedies.

Original Decca 78 rpm record album of songs from *The Wizard of Oz.*

While attending Townsend Harris Hall (which enrolled both high school and college students), Harburg befriended a young Ira Gershwin (1896–1983), who introduced him to the music of Gilbert and Sullivan. Lyricist W. S. Gilbert, who wrote the hilarious lyrics to the patter songs in their operettas, became Harburg's first idol. In later years, Harburg discovered the works of other literary wits, including George S. Kaufman, Dorothy Parker, and Marc Connelly, and he voraciously read Franklin P. Adams's "The Conning Tower," an influential column in the *New York World.*

After graduating from the City College of New York, Harburg wrote poetry and spent much time with Ira Gershwin, who had begun a lucrative career writing lyrics for his brother George's Broadway musicals. In 1929, inspired by Ira Gershwin's success, Harburg decided to try his hand at writing lyrics, and thanks to Ira's introduction, began writing songs with composer Jay Gorney (1894–1990). Before he settled into his partnership with Harold Arlen, Harburg wrote songs with 31 different composers. His breakthrough came in 1932 when he wrote lyrics to three revues, including *Americana,* for which Harburg and Gorney wrote one of the most evocative songs of the Depression years, "Brother, Can You Spare a Dime?" While working on *Americana,* Harburg met composer Harold Arlen, and although the two collaborated on just one inconsequential number for the revue ("Satan's Little

Lamb"), they worked together again throughout the decade, on the songs "It's Only a Paper Moon" (1932) and "Last Night When We Were Young" (1935), the revues *Life Begins at 8:40* (1934) and *The Show Is On* (1936), and the antiwar musical *Hooray for What!* (1937).

The Wizard of Oz was seen as M-G-M's answer to Walt Disney's 1937 commercial and critical triumph, *Snow White and the Seven Dwarfs.* When M-G-M announced that it would spare no expense in bringing Baum's famed children's book to the screen, many Hollywood songwriters eagerly anticipated being selected for the job. It was Arthur Freed (1894–1973), a former Tin Pan Alley lyricist writing songs for M-G-M films, who made the brilliant decision to hire Harburg and Arlen. Freed wanted to become a producer, so studio head Louis B. Mayer appointed him as assistant to *Oz* producer Mervyn LeRoy (1900–1987). After hearing Harburg and Arlen's work in *Hooray for What!*, Freed was convinced that the team was capable of writing whimsical songs with a nod toward sentimentality, which is what he had in mind for *Oz.* Freed later told actor Bert Lahr's son, John, "Harburg had a great sense of fantasy in his lyrics." After *Oz,* Harburg went on to write songs for other musicals featuring magical characters, including *Finian's Rainbow* and *Flahooley.*

Yip Harburg contributed more to *The Wizard of Oz* than just lyrics. In addition, he also had an influence on the screenplay, helping to manipulate the dialog so that it flowed more easily into the songs. It helped that the composers previously had worked with several of the key actors in the movie. In 1934, Bert Lahr (the Cowardly Lion) and Ray Bolger (the Scarecrow) appeared in Harburg and Arlen's Broadway revue *Life Begins at 8:40.* Two years later, Harburg and Arlen wrote a song for Lahr in another revue, *The Show Is On.* Buddy Ebsen, the original Tin Woodman, had also worked with Harburg, in the *Ziegfeld Follies of 1934.* (Ebsen was replaced in *Oz* by Jack Haley after Ebsen suffered a near-fatal allergic reaction to the aluminum dust used for his character's makeup.)

Harold Arlen

Harold Arlen (1905–1986) was born as Hyman Arluck in Buffalo, New York. The son of a cantor, he lived in a strict Orthodox Jewish home and learned to play piano and sing at an early age. While performing with a local group called the Buffalodians, he met dancer Ray Bolger, who would become one of his best friends.

Left to right: *Oz* songwriters E. Y. "Yip" Harburg and Harold Arlen, c. 1939.   MGM/Photofest

Despite a promising career as a jazz singer, it was as a composer that Arlen achieved his greatest acclaim. Beginning with "Get Happy" in 1929, he collaborated with lyricist Ted Koehler on many hit numbers and the two had a lucrative run as the house songwriting team for the Cotton Club in Harlem (1930–1934). During those years, they wrote such hits as "I Love a Parade," "I've Got the World on a String," and, most famously, "Stormy Weather," written for Ethel Waters. Arlen also wrote songs with other lyricists during this period, including Yip Harburg and Jack Yellen, and he also sang in revues at The Palace and Radio City Music Hall in Manhattan.

In 1934, the success of the Cotton Club was waning (it would close its doors for good in 1936), and Arlen split with Koehler to work with Harburg and Ira Gershwin on *Life Begins at 8:40.* The next year, Warner Brothers signed Harburg and Arlen to write the scores for three film musicals, and although they submitted some wonderful songs for these movies, none was commercially successful. In early 1938, after completing the score for *Hooray for What!,* Harburg and Arlen set to work on *The Wizard of Oz.* In May 1938, M-G-M signed them to a 14-week contract for a flat rate of $25,000. By the time they came on board, the script had gone through a number of revisions and was not yet finalized, which gave Harburg and Arlen the ability to write songs within the still developing storyline.

The Integrated Score

The songs for *The Wizard of Oz* were designed to be integrated into the story, a concept that was daring and ahead of its time in the late 1930s. Arthur Freed wanted song and dance to help define the characters and action in the film, not interrupt them in the fashion of most films and Broadway shows of the time. *The Wizard of Oz* wasn't the first production to do this (the 1927 Broadway musical *Show Boat* was the most noteworthy of early efforts employing an integrated score), but it was a landmark innovation for its time.

One of the most frequently asked questions of any songwriting team is, "Which comes first: the lyrics or the music?" In the case of Harburg and Arlen, Arlen typically wrote a part of the melody first, usually the first eight bars. From this, Harburg often invented a title and then Arlen would complete the melody, after which Harburg would finish writing the lyrics.

Producer Mervyn LeRoy (left), Judy Garland (center), and director Victor Fleming (holding Toto), on the set of Munchkinland.

MGM/Photofest

Roger Edens (1905–1970), one of M-G-M's music supervisors, designed the blueprint for some of Harburg and Arlen's songs, wrote some of the vocal arrangements, and had even written four songs himself, including one that the Munchkins would sing to Dorothy upon her arrival in Munchkinland. Although none of Edens's songs was used, his initial ideas inspired Harburg and Arlen to develop one of the most unique musical sequences in the film—a miniature operetta that included patter songs and rhymed dialog in a six-minute-long production number entitled "Munchkinland Musical Sequence."

Arlen referred to the first songs written for the film as "lemon-drop songs," those that were light and easy for him to compose. These included "Ding-Dong! The Witch Is Dead," "We're Off to See the Wizard" (originally titled "The Marching Song"), and "The Merry Old Land of Oz" (originally titled "Laugh a Day Away"). For the Scarecrow's solo, "If I Only Had a Brain," Arlen used a song that had been discarded from *Hooray for What!* titled "I'm Hanging On to You" and Harburg crafted different lyrics for each of Dorothy's three companions: the Scarecrow, the Tin Woodman, and the Cowardly Lion. Each of these three characters got a chance to sing the song, using the lyrics specified for each character.

Since both Ray Bolger and Jack Haley had more screen time than Bert Lahr in their renditions of "If I Only Had a Brain," Lahr was given his own specialty number, the only other solo showcase in the film, aside from Judy Garland's "Over the Rainbow." "If I Were King of the Forest," features Lahr spoofing the posturing baritones he had known in the theater. The style was one he was familiar with; "The Song of the Woodman" (from *The Show Is On*) and "Things" (from *Life Begins at 8:40*) were similar songs from revues in which Lahr brought down the house with his patented, punch-drunk vocal mannerisms.

During development, several songs were dropped from the production entirely, while others were altered or replaced by different songs. One of the songs that was taken out was "The Jitterbug," which was to have been sung by Dorothy and her companions, just prior to being menaced by the Winged Monkeys in the Haunted Forest while searching for the Wicked Witch. The song describes an insect set upon the quartet by the Witch that was supposed to give them "the jitters." Despite the fact that shooting the sequence had already cost $80,000 and consumed weeks of rehearsal and production time, M-G-M cut the number to save screen time. The decision to cut the song may have been a wise one because at that point in the movie, an upbeat, happy dance number could have been seen as going against the concept of an integrated film, where songs furthered the action. In this case, "The Jitterbug" might have spoiled the eery, spooky atmosphere of the scene in the Haunted Forest, and might not have added anything to the development of the story.

The word "jitterbug" also might have dated the film. The term had been popularized by bandleader Cab Calloway to describe swing dancers, whose frenetic movements suggested the effects of alcohol withdrawal (delirium tremens). Observant viewers will notice that the spoken cue for "The Jitterbug" number remains in the finished film. In the scene directly preceding what would have been the "Jitterbug" sequence, the Wicked Witch of the West (Margaret Hamilton) tells Nikko, the chief Winged Monkey (Pat Walshe), "Take your army to the Haunted Forest and bring me that girl and her dog. Do what you want with the others, but I want her alive and unharmed. They'll give you no trouble, I promise you that. I've sent a little insect on ahead to take the fight out of them." Despite being cut from the film, "The Jitterbug" was recorded by Judy Garland and included as the reverse side of her 1939 Decca recording of "Over the Rainbow."

There were other songs indicated in the various studio records. Many of these intriguing titles never

came to fruition, were deleted from the film, or were transformed into other songs. These include "Horse of a Different Color" (to be used in a scene inside the Emerald City), "Lions and Tigers and Bears" (which was reduced to a repeated chant), a reprise of "We're Off to See the Wizard" (replaced by "Optimistic Voices," sung by the quartet as they approached Emerald

Scene in the Haunted Forest, during which the song "The Jitterbug" was to be sung.   MGM/Photofest

City), and "Wizard Song" (to be sung by the Wizard while bestowing his gifts upon Dorothy's intrepid companions. This latter scene eventually was shot with dialog and "Gaudeamus Igitur" in the underscoring). A funeral march to be sung by the Winkies, "Death to the Wizard of Oz," was also dropped along with a subplot about the Witch's army conquering the Emerald City. The mystical chant from the song resurfaced as "The March of the Winkies." After the Wicked Witch is melted, Dorothy and her friends join in a triumphant parade, during which a medley of three *Oz* songs is played ("Ding-Dong! The Witch Is Dead," "The Merry Old Land of Oz," and "We're Off to See the Wizard"). This entire sequence, titled "Ding-Dong! Emerald City," was shot, but was deleted from the final film.

Over the Rainbow

Dorothy's character-defining moment comes in the first scenes of the film when she sings "Over the

Rainbow." In Baum's book, Dorothy is described as a little girl who has never seen anything beyond the gray Dust Bowl-weary Kansas landscape. Harburg reasoned that the only colorful thing she has ever seen in her life is a rainbow, so he decided to write a lyric in which Dorothy yearns to be someplace over that rainbow. For all his efforts, Arlen had trouble coming up with an appropriate melody to reflect Dorothy's feeling of frustration and yearning.

Unlike many composers, Harold Arlen usually didn't compose at the piano. Instead, he preferred to have inspiration strike him, which could occur anywhere at anytime. One day, he and his wife decided to go see a movie at Grauman's Chinese Theatre in Hollywood. While driving on Sunset Boulevard, they were about to pass the famous Schwab's Drugstore when a musical epiphany came to Arlen in the form of what he later

Judy Garland as Dorothy sings "Over the Rainbow."   MGM/Photofest

described as a "broad, long-lined melody." Arlen's wife pulled the car into a space on the curb directly opposite Schwab's so that Arlen could jot down the notes. According to Arlen, "It was as if the Lord said, 'Well, here it is, now stop worrying about it!'"

After Arlen came up with the opening of the song outside of Schwab's, he went home and developed that idea. The next day, he created the song's contrasting bridge, which he based on the idea of a child's piano exercise. When Harburg heard the song, however, he said that the melody was inappropriate for a poor little farm girl to sing. He explained that Dorothy was a girl

in trouble, but her troubles were those of a child, and the dramatic melody Arlen played just didn't suit her character. Arlen kept insisting that this was the right song for Dorothy to sing, but Harburg thought that the operatic octave jump in the first two notes of the chorus would be more appropriate for a more mature singer like Nelson Eddy. Frustrated, they asked Ira Gershwin for his opinion. After they performed it for him, Gershwin told Arlen to play the song with a little more rhythm and less drama, and the result worked to everyone's satisfaction. When Harburg and Arlen had trouble coming up with an ending for the song, Ira Gershwin suggested a tag with the lyrics: "If happy little bluebirds fly, why, oh, why, can't I?"

Harburg's lyrics mention things a little girl would dream of: lemon drops and lullabies, wishing upon stars, and flying bluebirds. His original dummy title for the song had been "Over the Rainbow Is Where I Want to Be," but he had trouble coming up with two syllables to match Arlen's octave jump at the start of the chorus. Eventually, he settled on adding the word "somewhere." He then wrote the dialog between Dorothy and her Aunt Em that led into the song.

When a preview of the movie was shown in San Bernardino in June 1939, some M-G-M producers suggested that the song slowed down the action and recommended dropping it. Other studio executives who saw the preview told Louis B. Mayer and producer Mervyn LeRoy that it was incongruous for an M-G-M star to be singing the song in the middle of a barnyard. Mayer agreed, and at the second preview in Pomona, it was removed from the film. By this time, Arthur Freed had begun production on *Babes in Arms,* the first film in which he acted as producer. The movie was to have a big budget and an all-star cast, featuring the high-energy duo of Garland and another highly touted young star, Mickey Rooney. Anticipation for the film's success was high, and as a result, Freed had now developed more clout than he had had when he started work on *Oz.* Freed and Mervyn LeRoy lobbied Mayer to return "Over the Rainbow" to the film, with Freed especially adamant about the song's value to the movie, telling Mayer "The song stays or I go." Mayer relented, and reinserted the song in the film, where it stayed. "Over the Rainbow" not only became the movie's biggest success, but it also won the Academy Award for Best Song for 1939. It has since become an enduring classic, one of the few songs in history introduced by a child that became a hit in the grown-up world.

Munchkinland

The Munchkinland scene was originally scripted in March 1938 by Herman Mankiewicz (1897–1953) as an elaborate multi-themed production number. (Mankiewicz worked on the film for only three weeks.) Many different ideas had been proposed for "Munchkinland," which included some songs written by Roger Edens. When Harburg and Arlen were hired a few months later, they expanded upon the idea, creating a six-minute-long musical sequence consisting of rhymed dialog and brief songs, patterned after the operettas of Gilbert and Sullivan. Harburg had experience writing in this form before, although only briefly, when he worked with Ira Gershwin on *Life Begins at 8:40.* That show's finale, which featured Bert Lahr, was a mock operetta titled "Beautifying the City" that included patter songs and reprises of numbers heard earlier in the show. In addition to writing the lyrics for "Munchkinland," Harburg also added the recitative dialog.

Original sheet music edition of "We're Off to See the Wizard."

The segment begins with the arrival of Glinda, the Good Witch (Billie Burke) and ends with Dorothy skipping down the Yellow Brick Road towards Oz. Except for a section of dialog when the Wicked Witch appears, the songs and recitative flow naturally, uninterrupted, as if in an operetta, and form what is one of the most unique and charming episodes of the entire film. Harburg's half-spoken/half-sung recitatives poke fun at the verbose pomposity of formal ceremonies, such as when the Town Council formally declares that the Wicked Witch of the East is "morally, ethically, spiritually, physically, positively, absolutely, undeniably, and reliably dead."

When it came time to record the soundtrack, the voices of almost all of the Munchkins were dubbed by professional session singers and altered in the studio by vocal arranger Ken Darby (1909–1992). To create the Munchkins' high-pitched voices, Darby added an extra gear to the recording equipment so that the voices could be recorded at a slower speed. (Recording tape had not yet been invented.) When played back at normal speed, this resulted in the cartoonish voices of the Munchkins. To make sure the words could be clearly understood, Darby had the actors enunciate their lines slowly and distinctly when the recordings were made. (Darby did the opposite when creating the low-pitched, menacing voices of the Winkie guards.) The sped-up vocals for "The Lullaby League" were dubbed by Lorraine Bridges, Betty Rome, and Carol Tevis, while "The Lollipop Guild" featured the voices of Billy Bletcher, Pinto Colvig, and Harry Stanton.

Herbert Stothart

Herbert Stothart (1885–1949) was assigned the job of adapting Harburg and Arlen's songs and composing a background score for *The Wizard of Oz.* The dean of the M-G-M music department, Stothart had a long history in Broadway before going to work for M-G-M. Among the many musical comedies he worked on as either a composer or conductor were *Rose-Marie* (with Rudolf Friml and Otto Harbach), *Wildflower* (with Oscar Hammerstein II), and the operetta *Song of the Flame* (with Hammerstein, Harbach, and George Gershwin). In 1929, Louis B. Mayer invited Stothart to join M-G-M as part of its music department, where he became a pioneer in the early years of orchestral scoring.

Stothart became M-G-M's principal music director, composing, arranging, and conducting music for more than 100 scores. From 1929 until his death in 1949, he worked with all of the studio's top directors and performers and developed a reputation for professionalism and the ability to inspire superior performances from his orchestras. In his work as musical director for *The Wizard of Oz,* Stothart created musical motifs to define the main characters in the movie and established the atmosphere necessary for scenes such as the cyclone and Dorothy's rescue from the Wicked Witch's castle. Assisting him was a team of renowned M-G-M orchestrators, which included George Bassman, George Stoll, and Robert Stringer. All of the orchestrations of the film's songs were prepared by Murray Cutter, except for the "Munchkinland Musical

Composer/conductor Herbert Stothart, shown in the M-G-M sound studio.　　MGM/Photofest

piano number often played by children. Stothart chose this piece to illustrate the bucolic life of the Gale family in Kansas. Other classical works Stothart used elsewhere in the film include Felix Mendelssohn's "Fantasy," op. 16, no. 2, to accompany Toto's escape from the Wicked Witch's castle ("Toto's Chase"), and a theme from Modeste Moussorgsky's *Night on Bald Mountain,* to accompany Dorothy's rescue from the castle ("Dorothy's Rescue"). Stothart sprinkled the soundtrack with other familiar quotations, such as the 1905 song "In the Shade of the Old Apple Tree" (for the scene in the apple orchard), the ancient commencement hymn "Gaudeamus Igitur" (for the scene where the Wizard bestows his gifts on the Scarecrow, the Tin Woodman, and the Cowardly Lion), the traditional children's song "Reuben and Rachel" (during the cyclone scene), and the 19th-century staple "Home Sweet Home" (for the final scene where Dorothy finally returns to Kansas).

Sequence," which was orchestrated by Leo Arnaud. (Conrad Salinger was responsible for the orchestration for the deleted "Jitterbug" number.)

Working on as many as a dozen films a year, Stothart often drew from a well that included quotations from familiar folk songs and classical music. Stothart's knowledge of concert works enabled him to become one of the most effective practitioners of incorporating classical themes into a film's underscore. His purpose in doing so was threefold: to expose film audiences to the world of classical music, to attract fans with more sophisticated musical tastes to the movies through his use of classical themes, and to attract concert composers to Hollywood. Stothart's ingenious score for *The Wizard of Oz* contains both touches of classical music and his own original themes that are as recognizable as any of the songs created by Harburg and Arlen. For his work on *Oz,* Stothart received the Academy Award for Best Original Score, chosen over Max Steiner's majestic music for *Gone With the Wind.*

Character Themes and Musical Cues

In the film's opening scene, which takes place on Dorothy's farm in Kansas, Stothart used a piece written by Robert Schumann called "The Happy Farmer," a

Stothart also wanted audiences to identify musically with each major character, so he created various musical motifs that were used throughout the film. Dorothy is linked with "Over the Rainbow," which she sings early on, and the Scarecrow, Tin Woodman, and Cowardly Lion are linked with "If I Only Had a Brain," however, when the Lion receives his medallion for courage from the Wizard, "If I Were King of the Forest" is played on the underscoring. The other characters, especially those who did not sing, posed a problem. As a result, Stothart composed brief instrumental themes for the important secondary characters of the Wicked Witch, Professor Marvel, and Glinda (The Good Witch). He also provided themes to represent the Emerald City and the Winkies army that guarded the Witch's castle.

The Wicked Witch's theme (titled "Miss Gulch: The Ultimate Witch") is first heard as the humorless school teacher Almira Gulch (Margaret Hamilton) bicycles along the road to the Gale farm. In creating the sinister tone for "Miss Gulch" (which was misspelled "Gultch" on the original conductor's score), Stothart composed a malevolent variation on the rhythm of Harburg and Arlen's cheery "We're Off to See the Wizard." The juxtaposition of these two rhythmically related tunes is meant to represent both the evil and benevolent sides of Oz. The rhythmic pattern of the theme gives the

Margaret Hamilton, during the scene where her theme, "Miss Gulch," is first heard.   MGM/Photofest

impression of movement, and thus amplifies the action of both of Hamilton's characters: Miss Gulch, riding her bicycle, and the Witch, riding her broom in the cyclone scene. The transformation of Miss Gulch to the Witch during this scene serves to link the two characters visually as well as musically. The theme recurs each time the Witch appears in a scene.

Character actor Frank Morgan plays six roles in *The Wizard of Oz:* Professor Marvel, the Wizard, the Emerald City gatekeeper, the carriage driver, the Wizard's guard, and the Great Head in the throne room, however, only two of these roles are shared by a single unifying melody: Professor Marvel and the Wizard. When Dorothy encounters Professor Marvel prior to the cyclone scene, the professor invites the young runaway into his wagon to foretell her future in his crystal ball. It is then that we first hear Herbert Stothart's mystical, oriental-tinged melody ("Crystal Gazing"). This theme is repeated in a later scene, when the Wizard dispenses his gifts to Dorothy's friends, thus linking the two characters.

"Glinda's Theme" is a repeated six-note phrase that accompanies the Good Witch's three appearances in the film (in Munchkinland, casting the curative spell over the poppy field, and in Emerald City). The brief

melody is the first music heard on the soundtrack (in the overture over the opening credits), and the first music heard after Dorothy's last line ("Oh, Auntie Em, there's no place like home!"), indicating the importance of Glinda as the true, omnipotent power of Oz.

Other significant cues composed by Stothart include two marches: "Change of the Guard" (the majestic theme for the Emerald City, which was co-written by George Bassman) and "March of the Winkies" (the dark, mysterious chant of the Witch's guards, which consists of the nonsensical syllables "O-Ee-Yah! Eoh-Ah!").

The 1903 Broadway Show

The Broadway version of *The Wizard of Oz,* with book and lyrics by L. Frank Baum and music by Paul Tietjens, had its premiere on June 16, 1902, at the Grand Opera House in Chicago. It was an instant hit and made stars of David Montgomery (the Tin Woodman) and Fred Stone (the Scarecrow). On January 21, 1903, the show opened at the Majestic Theatre in New York City. The Broadway production was the year's biggest hit, running for nine months. A successful road tour followed, and the musical returned to New York several times before its run ended in 1909. Stock and amateur companies continued to present it into the 1930s, when it was finally overshadowed by the classic M-G-M film starring Judy Garland.

Cary Ginell
Popular Music Editor
Alfred Music Publishing Co., Inc.

14

Rehearsal for the "Good News" radio program, June 29, 1939. Standing, left to right: Bert Lahr, Ray Bolger, M-G-M executive L. K. Sidney, Yip Harburg, composer Meredith Willson, music publisher Harry Link. Seated at the piano: Judy Garland and Harold Arlen.

MGM/Photofest

L. Frank Baum (1856–1919), author of *The Wizard of Oz* and lyricist for the 1903 Broadway production.

Photo courtesy of David Maxine.

"Over the Rainbow."

The Lollipop Kids, during the Munchkinland sequence.   MGM/Photofest
Left to right: Harry Doll, Jerry Maren, and Jackie Gerlich.

"We Welcome You to Munchkinland."

Judy Garland and the Munchkins.   MGM/Photofest

The Lullaby League ballerinas, with Judy Garland, during the Munchkinland sequence.   MGM/Photofest

"Follow the Yellow Brick Road." MGM/Photofest

Ray Bolger as the Scarecrow.   The John Fricke Collection

"We're Off to See the Wizard."

"If I Only Had a Heart."

Bert Lahr as the Cowardly Lion.   The John Fricke Collection

Left to right: Ray Bolger, Jack Haley, Judy Garland, and Bert Lahr exit the poppy field to "Optimistic Voices." MGM/Photofest

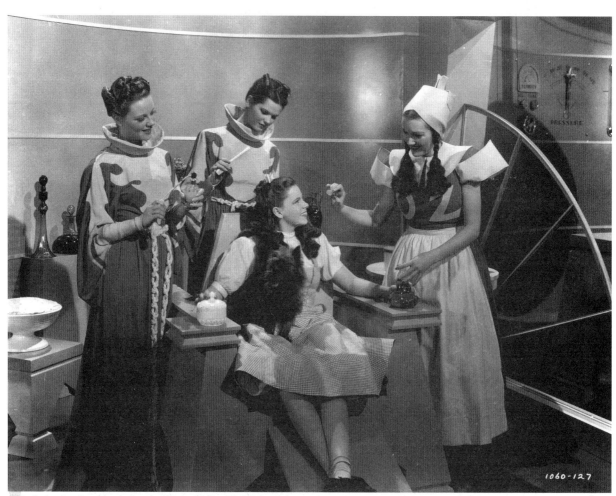

Judy Garland as Dorothy during the "Merry Old Land of Oz" sequence.
The manicurists are Dorothy Barrett, Lois January, and Ethelreda Leopold.

MGM/Photofest

Bert Lahr, as the Cowardly Lion, sings "If I Were King of the Forest."   MGM/Photofest

Margaret Hamilton
as the Wicked Witch
of the West.　　　　MGM/Photofest

Billie Burke as Glinda, the Good Witch of the North.　　　MGM/Photofest

Frank Morgan as the Wizard,　　　MGM/Photofest
one of six roles he played in
The Wizard of Oz.

OVER THE RAINBOW

Track 2: Demo
Track 3: Play Along

Music by
HAROLD ARLEN

COME OUT, COME OUT.../
IT REALLY WAS NO MIRACLE

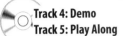
Track 4: Demo
Track 5: Play Along

Music by
HAROLD ARLEN

Come Out, Come Out.../It Really Was No Miracle - 2 - 1
33948

44 *"It Really Was No Miracle"*

DING-DONG! THE WITCH IS DEAD

Track 6: Demo
Track 7: Play Along

Music by
HAROLD ARLEN

Ding-Dong! The Witch Is Dead - 2 - 1
33948

THE LULLABY LEAGUE/
THE LOLLIPOP GUILD/
WE WELCOME YOU TO MUNCHKINLAND

Track 8: Demo
Track 9: Play Along

Music by
HAROLD ARLEN

33948

FOLLOW THE YELLOW BRICK ROAD/
WE'RE OFF TO SEE THE WIZARD

Track 10: Demo
Track 11: Play Along

Music by
HAROLD ARLEN

IF I ONLY HAD A BRAIN

Music by
HAROLD ARLEN

OPTIMISTIC VOICES

Music by
HAROLD ARLEN and
HERBERT STOTHART

Moderately bright ♩ = 104

THE MERRY OLD LAND OF OZ

Track 16: Demo
Track 17: Play Along

Music by
HAROLD ARLEN

With spirit ♩ = 96

THE JITTERBUG

Music by
HAROLD ARLEN

© 1938 (Renewed) METRO-GOLDWYN-MAYER INC.
© 1939 (Renewed) EMI FEIST CATALOG INC.
Rights Throughout the World Controlled by EMI FEIST CATALOG INC. (Publishing) and ALFRED MUSIC PUBLISHING CO., INC. (Print)
33948

IF I WERE KING OF THE FOREST

Track 20: Demo
Track 21: Play Along

Music by
HAROLD ARLEN

PARTS OF AN ALTO SAXOPHONE AND FINGERING CHART

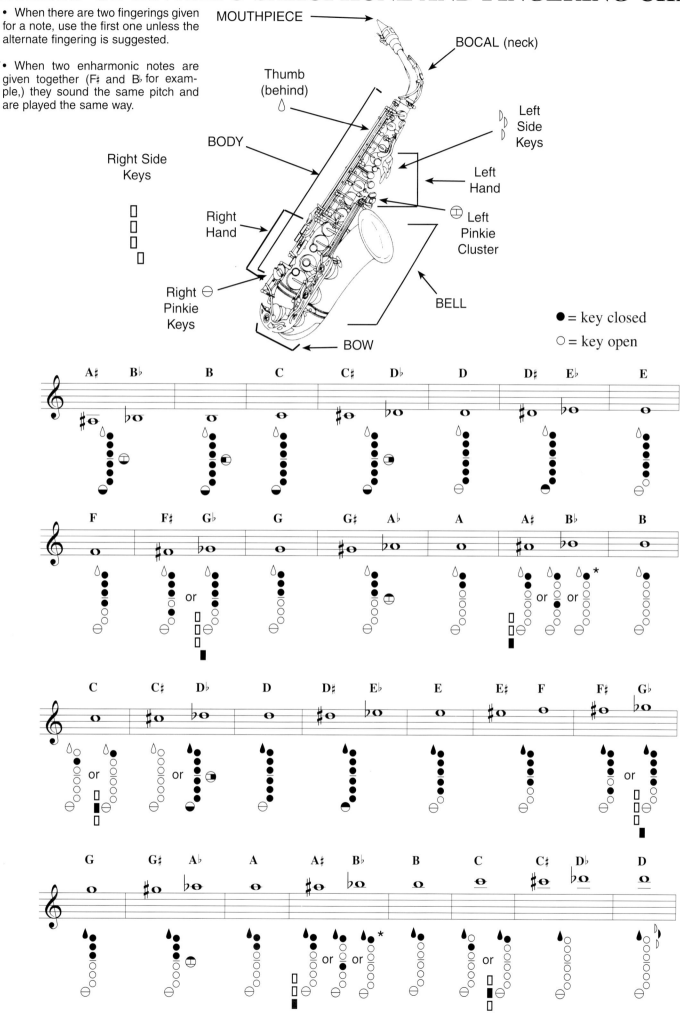

• When there are two fingerings given for a note, use the first one unless the alternate fingering is suggested.

• When two enharmonic notes are given together (F♯ and B♭ for example,) they sound the same pitch and are played the same way.

* Both pearl keys are pressed with the Left Hand 1st finger.

Alfred